Sophia's BeeFF

Richard Irvine & Rachel Hoo

For

Sophia

and

Ellie

There are friends.
There are best friends.
Then there's the gold star,
world champion, most awesome,
best-est, best friend of all.
The Best Friend FOREVER!
The BFF.

And for this little girl, Sophia is
her name, her BFF is…

a bee.

Honey

Now, this particular bee is a
honey bee.
And this particular honey bee is
a girl bee, if you know what
I mean?
Not everyone can spot the
difference, but Sophia can.

"Girl bees may be smaller than
boys," she will tell you,
"But it's the girls, not the boys,
who have…

THE STINGERS!

So next time you pick a fight with a bee,
Hope that it's a boy, not a girl.

As interesting as this is,
it's not why Sophia and
the bee are BFF's.

You see, like all BFF's,
they agree on all the
important stuff like…

...dancing.

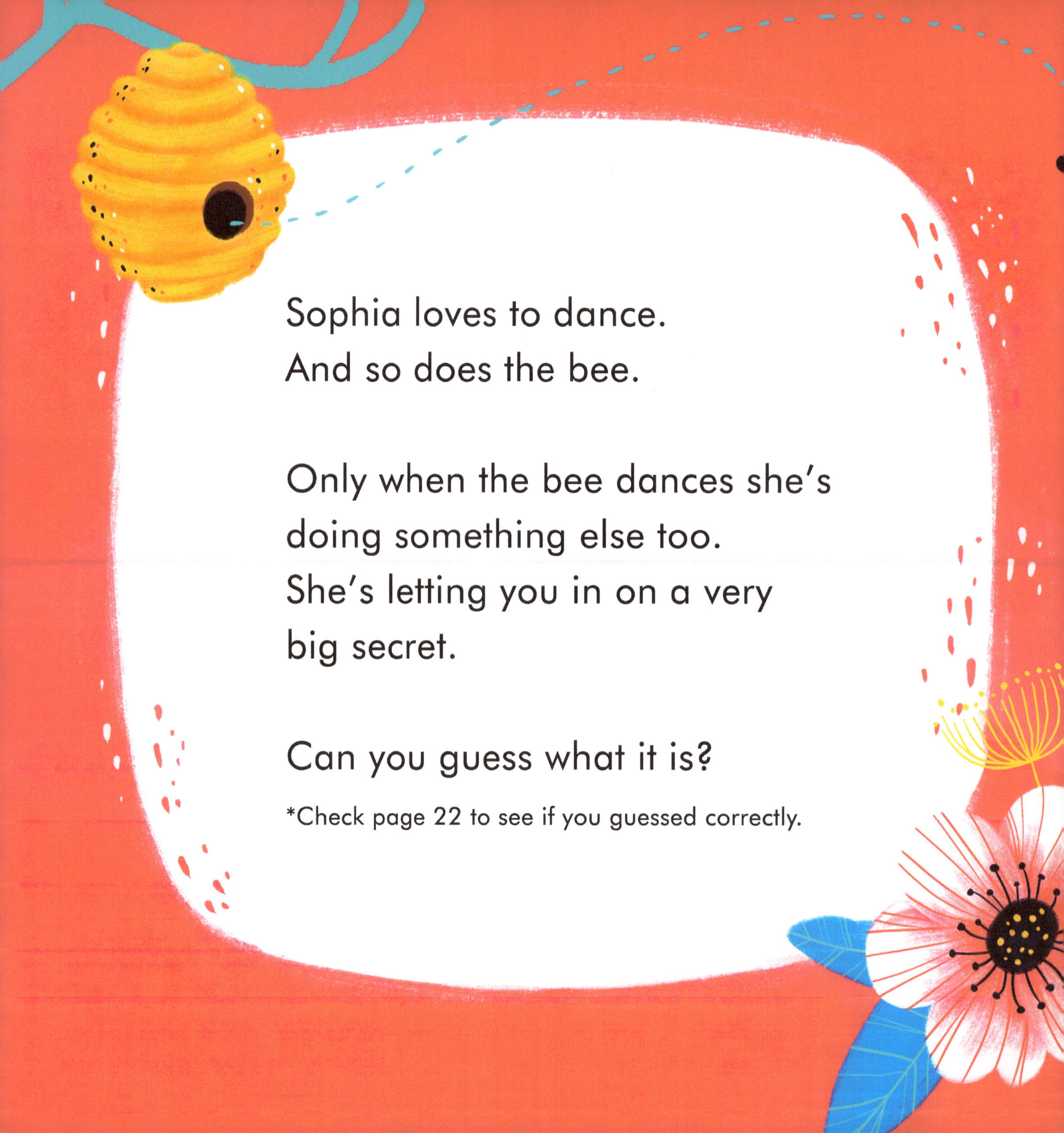

Sophia loves to dance.
And so does the bee.

Only when the bee dances she's
doing something else too.
She's letting you in on a very
big secret.

Can you guess what it is?

*Check page 22 to see if you guessed correctly.

Waggle
Waggle

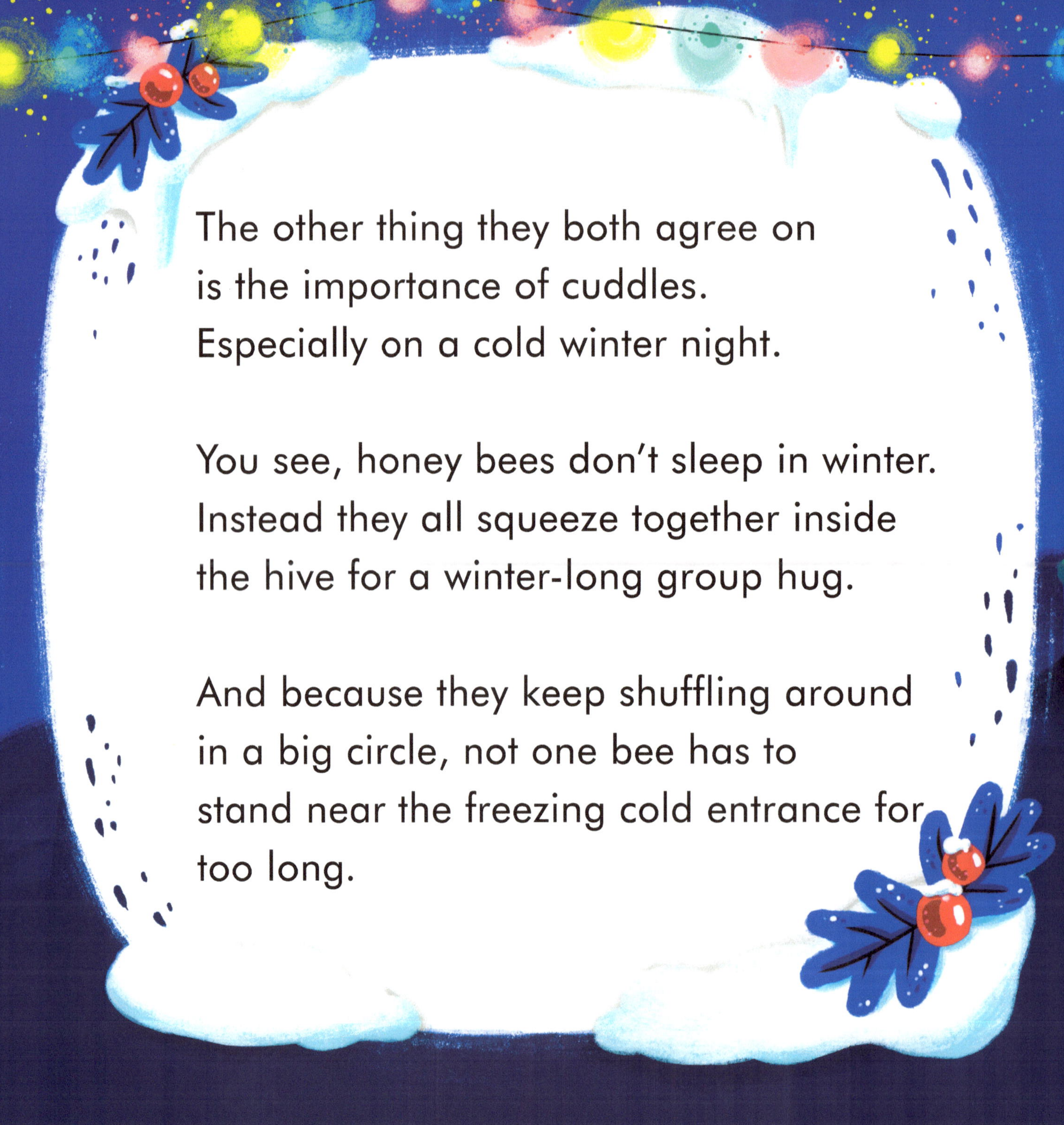

The other thing they both agree on
is the importance of cuddles.
Especially on a cold winter night.

You see, honey bees don't sleep in winter.
Instead they all squeeze together inside
the hive for a winter-long group hug.

And because they keep shuffling around
in a big circle, not one bee has to
stand near the freezing cold entrance for
too long.

Finally, they both enjoy giving gifts.
The bee is quite an expert on gifting.
From beeswax candles to soap, to shiny lip
balm, to delicious honey and all kinds of
medicines that help poorly people get better.

In return Sophia leaves out a saucer of water
for her BFF. Which may not seem much to
you and me, but to a bee, it really is a very
thoughtful gift. The bees knees you might say.

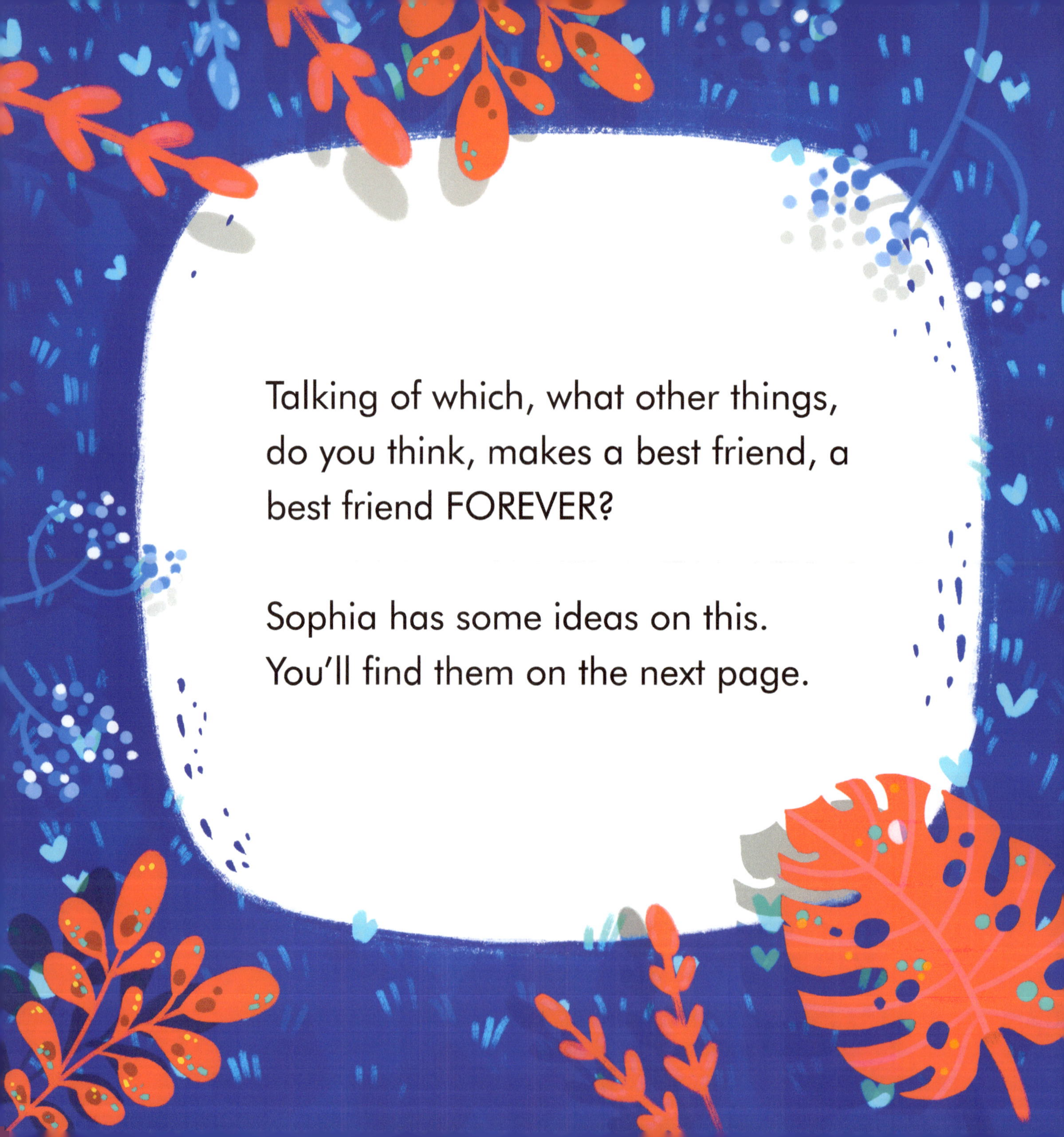
Talking of which, what other things, do you think, makes a best friend, a best friend FOREVER?

Sophia has some ideas on this. You'll find them on the next page.

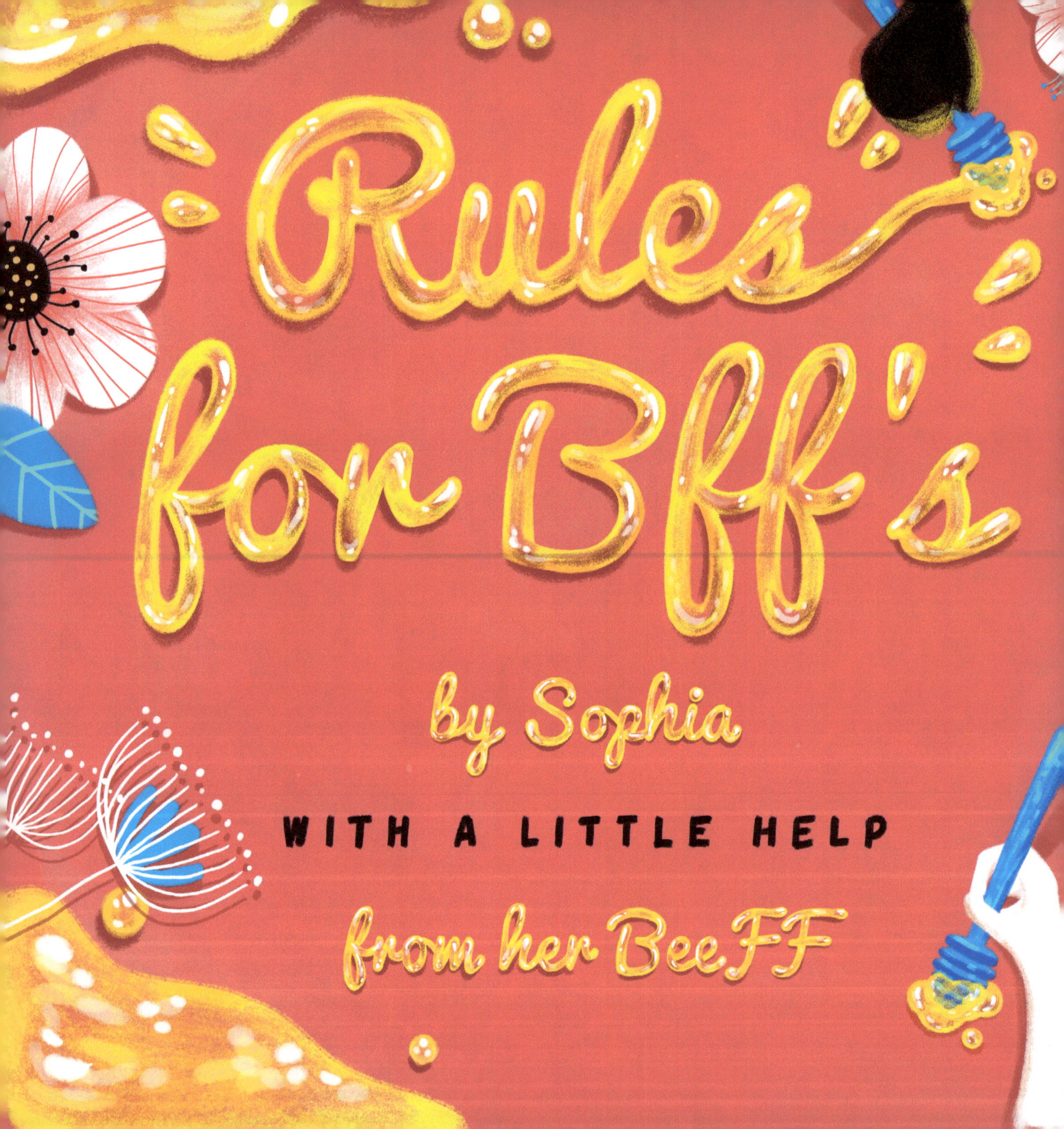

Rules for Bff's
by Sophia
WITH A LITTLE HELP
from her BeeFF

Bee Loyal

Always stand by your BFF even if sometimes it makes you unpopular with others.

Bee Considerate

Don't always think about what you want.
The wishes of your BFF are just as important.

Bee Honest

Neither tell fibs about your BFF or to your BFF.
No good will come of it.

Bee Suportive

If your BFF is going through a tough time,
or they just need some encouragement at school,
be their cheer leader.

Bee Forgiving

Even BFF's occasionally use hurtful words. If this happens to you, be the first to forgive and forget.

Author's Note

Bees truly are wonderful creatures and help us humans in more ways than we can possibly imagine. They really are our best friends forever. If you would like to learn a little bit more about these fascinating insects read on.

Girls v boys: Although the female bees do the bulk of the work, and are in fact called "Worker Bees," the males, called "Drones", are not lying around all day in the hive playing video games (although I'm sure they would love to). No, they also have important jobs to do like helping the Queen Bee make babies, tidying up the hive and taking out the rubbish. Maybe they should be called House Bees, not Drones?

To dance is to talk: When a worker bee dances the Waggle Dance (seriously, that's what it's called), she's actually telling her fellow bees where, and just how far, the flowers with the best quality nectar and pollen, can be found. It's these two ingredients that the bees use to make honey. By moving from flower to flower the bees also help the flowers cross-pollinate. Which means more flowers will grow in more places more often. A double bonus!

That's a long way to fly for a jar of honey: To collect enough pollen and nectar to make just 1 jar of honey, 200 bees have to visit 6 million flowers. Imagine that? That's the same as 1 bee flying all the way around the world!

Shiver and keep warm: In addition to huddling together and moving around in a big circle during the cold winter nights, the bees use the muscles that power their wings to shiver. All this shivering raises the temperature inside the hive to a cozy 35° centigrade. How cool…er…warm is that?

The gift of water: Just like humans, bees get thirsty and nothing quenches their thirst quite like a nice sip of water. Only bees can't swim, which makes drinking from a river or a pool quite dangerous. This is where you can help. Take a saucer, place a few pebbles in the bottom, add water and put it in your garden. The bees can then stand on the pebbles and drink without fear of falling in.

The precious properties of propolis: Everyone knows that bees make honey but did you know that bees also produce a magical sticky brown substance called propolis? Such a difficult word to pronounce, isn't it? So try saying it like this: PROP-O-LIS. Propolis is good at killing bad germs and the bees use it to protect their hive from disease. People can use it too to help heal cuts, sooth sore throats and prevent pesky colds.

The End